Evocations for Beginners

History, Experiences, Analysis and Methods

Contact: www.HarryEilenstein.de
Harry.Eilenstein@web.de
Harry Eilenstein at youtube

Production and publishing: BoD - Books on Demand, Norderstedt

ISBN: 9783753454344

Table of Contents

I What is an Evocation?

Evocations are probably the area of magic that is most creepy for most people – summoning demons at midnight at a crossroads … or even worse: summoning the spirits of the dead from their graves!

Even in commonly known literature such conjurations do not have a good reputation: Thus in "Lord of the Rings" Sauron appears as a necromancer who has conjured the spirits of nine deceased kings to serve him as "Black Riders".

One thing is for sure: This is black magic!

However, it is worthwhile (as with all things) to take a closer look at what such an evocation of a demon or such an evocation of a dead person actually is.

During an evocation a being, which has no own body (any more), becomes physically visible – optimally it has thereby the "consistency of dense vapors", as Frater Thot, my former colleague in the magic research, has described this aptly.

What is wrong with wanting to see a being that has no body of its own? And that one possibly wants to talk to?

Of course, if one assumes that the price for the help one wants to obtain from the demon or the dead is one's own soul, the matter is more than delicate. However, the question arises whether it is even possible to lose one's own soul – isn't it, with its abilities, very likely above anything we humans can do?

In the ideas about demon incantations it is usually the devil himself to whom one sells one's soul – against power, earthly riches and the like. This gives rise to the well-founded initial suspicion that the bad reputation of the incantations has something to do with the Christian church – after all, the devil is part of Christian mythology.

This connection suggests to take a closer look at the evocations of spirits in other cultures as well as at the relation of evocations to other magical-spiritual methods.

II   The Environment of Evocation

If one takes a closer look, one can see that evocation has quite a large environment of similar methods, some of which have quite a different reputation than demon evocations.

II 1.   Evocation and Dream Journey

What is the essence of an evocation? Why does one perform an evocation? As a rule, in order to meet a spirit, to speak with it and to receive something from it – as a rule, an advice, a help, a shaping of life circumstances and the like.

If we compare a dream journey with an evocation, we can see that both are actually very similar: also in a dream journey we meet various non-material beings from whom we can receive advice and help.

The difference between an evocation and a dream journey is essentially that in the evocation one summons the spirit and it appears in the outer material world, while in the dream journey one goes to the spirit and sees it in the inner world of consciousness.

Both are encounters with a spirit and in both methods the dream traveler in most cases seeks advice and help from the spirit. The difference is only the place where one meets – and the very different reputation of the two methods …

II 2.   Evocation and Vision

In an evocation, one invites the spirit to come to one – but it also works the other way around, i.e. the spirit can also decide to come to visit the person. And then there are the cases when both simply meet more or less by chance.

The visit of a spirit unintentionally by oneself would probably be called "vision". Here one sees the spirit as part of the perception of the external world – the image of the spirit is integrated into the optical perception. One then has a combined perception of an external image and an internal image.

A psychologist would probably call such a thing a psychosis and recommend therapy – but it makes a big difference whether one can clearly differentiate between the part of the inner images in the outer images or whether one thinks the whole outer/inner image is the outer reality. Only in the second case there will be problems –

in the first case the "additional inner pictures" can be an enrichment throughout.

A vision is consequently a medieval form of "augmented reality" …

Strictly speaking, an evocation can be called an "intentionally induced vision". You see a spirit, you talk to it and you possibly receive advice and help from it – this is exactly the same as with a vision.

Since in a dream journey (only inner images) and in a vision (integration of an inner image into the outer images) one not only sees and hears something, but can also smell, touch, taste and feel temperatures, there is no difference in principle between both types of perception – both can seem equally "real".

Both are actually equally "real" – both have an inner reality, both are real in the realm of consciousness – and can also have an effect on the outside.

II 3.   Evocation and Medium

It is not so easy to see an inner image also on the outside – which is also quite good, because thereby the perception of the outer reality remains stable.

However, since there have been repeated attempts to contact spirits, people have been looking for ways to build bridges from the "spirit realm" to the "human realm". One of these methods is the medium.

In some cases, the medium puts himself in a "receptive state" where a spirit can speak through the medium – in other cases, a hypnotist/magician puts the medium in this state. There are mediums who consciously experience everything they say and possibly do during their trance – other mediums are during their trance like a hypnotized person without waking consciousness and consequently without memory, i.e. they do not know afterwards what they have said and possibly done.

The task of the hypnotist/magician in this context is to "switch off" the waking consciousness of the medium.

In the case of a medium, therefore, the called spirit does not manifest itself outside the people involved as images and words in space, but only through the words and deeds of the medium.

II 4.   Evocation and Otherworld Journey

If the spirit that is to be called is a deceased person, one can also undertake an afterlife journey and go to visit the spirit at its new "place of residence", so to speak.

Such an afterlife journey can be a simple dream journey, but also an astral journey, in which the one who calls the spirit leaves his body and travels into the afterlife. As a rule, however, it will be a dream journey and not an experience similar to a near-death.

II 5.   Evocation and Apparitions of Mary

In Christianity many apparitions of Mary have been reported – much more rarely also apparitions of other saints. Sometimes Mary has been seen by larger groups of people at the same time. Similar phenomena exist in other religions as well.

If one wishes, one can call a Marian apparition a spontaneous evocation of Mary – or a vision.

This kind of phenomenon raises the question of its reality:

> - Does it take place only in the psyche of the visionary?
> > The visions that several people have at the same time speak against it. The minimal assumption in this case is that this visionary group is telepathically closely connected – similar to a joint dream journey of several persons.

> - Does this phenomenon take place only in the telepathically coordinated psyches of the visionary group?
> > If the visionary being promises e.g. a healing and this also occurs, one must at least assume a kind of telekinesis or a great power of the consciousness of the sick person over his body. In both cases it results that the visionary group as a whole has a great formative power.
> > If several 10,000 people see the apparition at the same time, the idea of a telepathically coordinated group of people is still conceivable, but one should assume that something which more than 10,000 people telepathically perceive at the same time acquires a form of independence which is more than just a joint vision …

- How real is the appeared being?

In several cases the apparition of Mary has been photographed. So the apparition must have actually existed on the outside, or a well-coordinated collective telekinesis must have transferred the image that everyone saw to the film in the camera as well.

If the visionary being does something that is external to the human being (other than a healing), such as an object materializing or changing, there are still the two interpretations that this was done by Mary (in the case of a Marian apparition) or that it was done by collective telekinesis capable of materialization.

These two models are still different, but the difference is no longer very big. It reduces to the question whether in the example Mary is an image in the psyches of the people or whether Mary has an independent existence.

This is the same question as the one about the nature of the collective subconsciousness: Are the archetypes in the collective subconsciousness only the telepathic union of the images in the psyches of the people or do these archetypes have a momentum of their own and an independent existence, i.e. are they deities in the conventional sense?

The same question about the reality of the beings that can appear as visions arises in the case of an evocation: What are these conjured spirits?

The answer is the same as in the case of the apparitions of Mary: They are archetypes in the collective subconscious and as such possess the abilities of telepathy and telekinesis … but the extent of their autonomy is still unclear for the time being.

II 6.   Evocation and Cult of the Dead

This consideration is less concerned with the question of the reality of the beings who may appear in evocation or as visions, than with the question of the relationship of human beings to these beings.

The cult of the dead is actually a misleading name. In the earlier cults at the time when there were no schools and no health insurance, no libraries and no pension rights, the family was the only support of the individual – especially one's parents. If the parents had died, one naturally felt the need to continue to receive advice and help from them. So one undertook dream journeys to them, one devised oracles through which one could speak with the ancestors, one made offerings of gratitude to them, etc.

The "inner conversation" with the deceased, which could also become a real dream journey, was thus something extremely natural – the normal behavior of a human being, so to speak.

There is another interesting point here, which is related to the idea one has about the soul and its destiny after death. If one has once experienced an astral journey during a near-death, i.e. has left his material body with his own life-force body, one can at least no longer claim with certainty that people cease to exist at their death.

This means that the dead possibly continue to exist as a soul (astral body) after their death. If one now calls upon the dead and asks for advice and help – does one then only have to do with one's own memory of these dead or with the souls of these dead?

Strictly speaking, one cannot really know – but for all pragmatic purposes one can pretend to speak with the souls of the dead …

II 7. Evocation and Invocation

The difference between these two magical methods is not very great – or it is very great … depending on whether one considers the congruence or the difference of the two methods the more important.

With an evocation one calls a spirit being in front of oneself in order to speak with it – with an invocation one calls a spirit being into oneself in order to be able to participate in its properties and abilities.

Both have in common that one calls a spirit being, thus a being without material body, and that this being then also appears. The difference is that in the evocation one keeps a distance to this being, while in the invocation one unites with this being.

The question about the reality of the called spirit-being is the same in both cases. If it is only a question of whether these two methods bring the desired success (i.e. advice and help), the question of the reality of these beings is secondary.

II 8. Evocation and Poltergeist

Poltergeists show themselves by footsteps on the stairs, words in the night, various noises and of course by occasional loud rumbling.

Sometimes also telekinetic phenomena occur in this context. I know of two occasions in which the poltergeist draw away the bedspread of a person who tried to sleep – that can be rather annoying …

Poltergeists appear almost exclusively in two contexts: first, as a concomitant of a teenager's difficult puberty, and second, in very old buildings. The "puberty poltergeists" suggest an interpretation of these phenomena as uncontrolled telekinesis of the pubescent, who has a great inner stress. The "castle poltergeists" are generally interpreted as "restless dead". In many cases they can also be traced back to people who have committed suicide.

The rumbling, i.e. the "not physically generated sounds" are obviously a telekinetically generated phenomenon – either by a living person or by a dead person. These sounds are sometimes rather loud.

II 9. Evocation and Exorcism

Exorcism is the counterpart of an invocation or the therapy of an unsuccessful evocation, in which the called spirit has taken over the magician, i.e. has hypnotized the magician, so to speak. The magician, whose waking consciousness has been "switched off" by the spirit, is "inhabited" by a spirit that has taken over the position of the magician's waking consciousness.

Actual possession by a spirit is rare – an unstable psyche, the emergence of a repressed part of the consciousness, or even psychosis are much more common, but this does not mean that there are no "real" possessions.

The obsession is sometimes simply a heightened case of unautonomy – by "unautonomy" is meant that the person concerned is still very strongly influenced by the inner image of his father, mother or another person and has not yet really freed himself from his own "family tradition". In extreme cases this can then look as if a person suddenly becomes "like his father" and behaves exactly like him – and at other times, however, again "be himself" and be completely "normal".

It is therefore better to be cautious and reserved with the diagnosis "possession" and the resulting therapy "exorcism".

II 10.   Evocation and Materialization

Materializations are one of the more extreme magical phenomena. If you have not experienced such a materialization yourself, it is hard to imagine that such a thing can really happen.

In combination with an evocation or the invocation of a deity such a materialization is of course very impressive. In any case, it shows that both the evocation of spirits and the invocation of deities have great power and can achieve a lot.

The materialization does not say much about the reality of the beings, which one calls during an evocation and which can appear then – in the end it becomes only obvious that one can release phenomena by an evocation, which clearly question the usual, purely material world view … which is of course already very much …

II 11.   Evocation and Spiritus familiaris

A Spiritus familiaris is a familiar spirit, i.e. a self-produced spirit. A proven recipe for it is:

> - Mix 2 parts of yellow clay with one part of beeswax, let the mixture melt in a pot on the stove and then form the body of the spirit out of it – e.g. a bear. Drill a hole at least 5 cm long in the body of the bear with a stick.
> - Make a decoction (very strong, almost pulpy tea) of chamomile flowers and add a few drops of Aurum chloratum C200 (a homeopathic remedy).
> - This brew as well as some drops of your blood is poured into the hole in the bear and the hole is closed with a plug of the clay/wax mixture.
> - Now give the spirit a name and henceforth address it by this name.
> - Hold the bear in one hand and with the other hand let life force flow into this spirit – the elements earth, water, air, fire and light.
> - One supplements this strengthening, if desired, by blood, menstrual blood, sperm and the like – substances rich in life force.
> - One asks, if desired, a deity (in this case a bear deity) for the strengthening of this spirit.

One can then send this spirit out to fulfill certain tasks – whereby with the selection of these tasks no borders are set to the fantasy.

This "house spirit" is obviously a creature that has been created as part of the magician's psyche – or formed out of the substance (life force) of the magician's psyche. To such a house spirit one develops a similar relationship as to a pet – only that the house spirit tends to become more independent. This finally leads to the fact that one must dissolve it again – what often feels like a self-amputation …

Such a house spirit can be sent off with the most different tasks without big evocation rituals – it is obviously closely connected with one's own psyche.

A house spirit is something like a self-produced ghost, wich is easy to call and direct – at least in the first time before it besomes more and more stronger and independant. So the forming of such a house spirit may be an alternative to the evocation of a spirit – but the procedure has also its drawbacks (like described above).

II 12. Evocation and Black Magic

Evocations are often attributed to black magic. However, this is not a very factual classification.

The question whether a magical act is "black" or "white" does not depend on the technique used, but on the motivation. And even the motivation of a person can still be evaluated differently – depending on the moral value standards of the evaluator.

Is calling the deceased father for help in a big crisis black magic? Or is summoning a Mars spirit to help one defend one's own life and family black magic?

Moreover, there are very rarely "only good people" or "only bad people". The rule case are the "good/evil-mixed people", who have only a limited self-knowledge and also only a limited overview and a limited ability to act. Therefore, there is almost nowhere White Magic and Black Magic, but almost only different shades of Gray Magic …

So it is recommended to look at what someone does and why – and then possibly to check if he has a clear motivation and if he has really chosen the most effective course of action …

This also applies to one's own actions – and to one's own evocations.

III   The Roots of Evocation

The evocation of spirits, especially the evocation of spirits of the dead has a long tradition. It therefore makes sense to take a closer look at the roots of evocation.

III 1.   Cult of the Dead

The most important root is certainly the cult of the dead. The living felt the need to continue to receive advice and help from their deceased parents and therefore sought ways to maintain contact with them even after their death.

To do this, the obvious thing to do was to go to the grave of the dead person with whom they wanted to speak. In some cultures, as for example with the earlier Chinese, one therefore built the death shrine directly in the house or at least directly beside the house – so that the dead were always in the proximity …

One tried in many ways to establish the contact to the dead as intensively as possible. So it was common until the Middle Ages to drink from the skull of the deceased to stay connected with him.

In Christianity, drinking from the skulls of the saints was widespread. The saints had certain functions, which were derived from their life: S. Jude Thaddeus against threat of violence, S. Adrain against the plague, S. Blaise against headache, S. Klara for telepathy and so on. Depending on the need one had, one could go on pilgrimage to the church where the skull of the saint in question was kept, and then drink from it.

Very similar customs are also known from the Buddhists in Tibet. The oldest skull drinking vessels that are known come from the Neolithic Age in Great Britain – although of course it is not known what idea people had at that time when drinking from these skulls.

Strictly speaking, this custom does not belong to the evocations, but to the invocations, since through this drinking people wanted to take into themselves the qualities of the sacred.

The drinking of Christ's blood at the Lord's Supper is a very similar symbolism … It is also found among many primitive peoples who, for example, by drinking the blood of the bear they have just killed, want to take into themselves the power of that bear.

These drinking traditions illustrate the relationship of people to the dead in the Middle Ages and even earlier times – death was not a taboo, but something that was dealt with quite naturally and pragmatically, and which was also included in magic.

So necromancy in the Middle Ages was nothing as sinister as it is today, when most people do not have a particularly relaxed relationship with death.

Cannibalism is a similar tradition: by eating the dead, one preserved its power in the clan. This custom once existed not only in faraway islands with palmtrees, but also among the Indo-Europeans (Scythians and others) and the early Egyptians.

III 2. Necromancy

"Necromancy" means precisely translated "divination with the help of the dead." In general, necromancy is also called "evocation of the dead" – simply because the dead were summoned in order to learn from them something about the future, about difficult situations, and the like.

The evocation of the dead was therefore once a normal oracle method – just like the tarot cards, the I Ching or astrology today.

III 3. Spiritism

Spiritism is an oracle method that goes back to the tradition of invoking the dead.

In spiritism either a medium is used, through which the dead person speaks, or a Quija board, i.e. a board on which the alphabet, the numbers from 0 to 9 as well as "yes" and "no" are written. Through various methods, the participants now select letters and numbers one after the other, which then represent the answers of the dead.

The most common method is the glass moving: A glass is placed on the board with its opening facing down. All persons present place a finger on this glass. Through the unconscious movements of the arms, the glass then moves around on the board. This method can be seen as a "collective pendulum". In this way, information can be obtained telepathically that is not known to any of the participants – and also "meaningful coincidences" can be evoked.

During spiritualistic sessions telekinetic phenomena or materializations often occur.

The difference with evocation is mainly that the conversation with the dead in Spiritism has been mechanized – but the accompanying magical effects are the same as in evocation: telepathy, telekinesis and materializations.

III 4.   Utiseta and Necromancy

Western evocation has not only Christian roots. The Germanic people so often called upon their ancestors for advice and help that there was a fixed term for it: "utiseta", i.e. "sitting outside". They called the dead out of their graves or tumuli and then talked to them.

The Celts, the Slavs, the Romans and the Greeks also had similar traditions.

The necromancy can be traced back to the early Neolithic period.

At that time, a mound of brushwood or stones and earth was erected over the grave, representing the belly of the earth goddess who was pregnant with the dead person, whom she would then give birth to in the afterlife. These mounds corresponded to the sweat lodge, in use since the Paleolithic period, which also represented the belly of the Great Mother.

In order to contact the dead, one sat on their mound grave. From this mound-symbolism a variety of traditions arose:

- The seers of the Germanic tribes sat on a pedestal when they wanted to make contact with the ancestors and learn about the future from them.
- The druids of the Celts sat down on a mesh of rowan branches when they sought connection with the gods and the ancestors.
- The Indians sat down to meditate (which has been derived from the afterlife journey) on a rock covered with a fur. The gods of the Indians instead sit on a lotus flower.
- The shamans of Harrappa and Mohenjo Daro in western India also sat on a pedestal for the afterlife journey.
- The Sem priests (shamans) of the Egyptians sat on a flat table when they traveled to the afterlife for burial to bring the soul of the deceased into his statue so that it would be with their descendants.

All these pedestals, stools, tables and so on are symbols of the mound of the dead. Nothing remains of this very ancient custom in the medieval evocation tradition.

III 5. Family Constellations

A modern variant of necromancy is the family constellation, which has been adopted from the cult of the dead in South Africa.

In this magical-psychological method, some of the participants take on the role of a "conscious medium".

The person who wants to clarify a question with the help of a constellation briefly presents this question. Then the leader looks at which persons have an importance for this question: e.g. the constellator, his father, his sister etc.. Then the leader asks who wants to represent which of these persons. When all roles are filled, the actors stand on a designated area (a large carpet, the center of the room, or the like).

Now the actors, who know almost nothing about the person they are portraying, intuitively move around the room and occasionally say something. In doing so, they exactly match the character of the person they are portraying, although they know nothing about them – they "channel" this person. They are then e.g. spontaneously just as choleric as the grandfather and also limp like him. Also the relationship of the portrayed persons among themselves is exactly reproduced by the actors – without them knowing anything about it. The actors even recognize family secrets and other things that even the questioner did not know about.

Through the actions and the conversations that take place among the actors (i.e. actually between the persons portrayed), for example, old quarrels can be settled, feelings of guilt and thoughts of revenge can be resolved. In this way, peace can return to the family – even among the family members who know nothing at all about the fact that a person from their family has carried out such a constellation.

A family constellation is a perfect summoning of a whole series of dead people from the clan by the volunteers who have made themselves available as a medium for these dead people (and sometimes also for people who are still alive).

If the "systemic family constellation" had the somewhat more traditional name of "collective necromancy", it would certainly not have been as well integrated as it has become …

IV   The Evocation in Christianity

The importance of the evocation of the dead, especially among the Germanic peoples and to some extent also among the Celts and the Slavs, has had a very strong influence on the development of Christianity in the missionization of Western, Northern, Central and Eastern Europe.

IV 1.   Father and God Father

Parents were the most important support for the Germanic people – even after their death. When the missionaries wanted to bring Christianity to them and told them about the one God Father in the afterlife, the Germanic people already had their own dead fathers in the afterlife to help them. Why should they exchange their own father for the one God Father of the Christians, unknown to them?

This was a serious problem for the missionaries …

IV 2.   The Devil

In order to get the Germanic people to turn to the Christian God Father and not to their own father, the missionaries had to argue against the dead in the afterlife and present them as a threat. They were helped in this by the general fear of death and also by the fact that the Germanic peoples had become uncertain in their religious ideas, partly due to internal upheavals in their religion (deposition of Tyr by Odin around 500 A.D.).

Already in the late Paleolithic Age there was the idea that the arrival in the hereafter corresponded to the arrival in this world, i.e. that it was a second birth, a "rebirth". Such a rebirth, of course, had to be preceded by a re-conception and followed by a re-feeding. The rebirth is of course a purely male motive …

This motive implicated that the men wanted to secure their procreative power in the hereafter. What to do? The greatest procreative power had apparently the herd-animals (since they appeared in large flocks), thus the cattle, deer, horses, pigs, sheep and goats. Therefore, a deer, a bull, a stallion, a boar, a ram or a he-goat was sacrificed for the dead person and then the dead person was wrapped in the hide of the sacrificial animal in order to transfer its procreative power to the dead man.

In this way, the dead men in the afterlife also took on the form of the male herd animal in question. The Great Mother, as the procreation lover, rebirth mother and nursemaid of the dead, then took the form of the corresponding female herd animal: hind, cow, mare, sow, sheep and goat. Since the dead man still retained his human form in spite of this herd-animal magic, he became in the afterlife a man with deer antlers, a minotaur, a centaur, a boar-man, a man with ram horns, or a faun.

These man/herd-animal hybrids the missionaries took as a starting point for their argumentation that the ancestors in the hereafter are something evil – although of course they will not have mentioned the ancestors so directly, since nobody will have regarded his father as the evil par excellence. In this way, the devil with his goat horns and with his horse's foot came into being – he is the reinterpreted dead father in the hereafter, who was partly transformed into a herd animal by the herd animal magic.

IV 3. The Devil's Grandmother

The second important figure in the afterlife, besides the dead man himself, was the Great Goddess, with whom the dead man procreated himself and who then re-birthed him and nursed him again.

Now, of course, it was hardly possible to reinterpret the mother, who is, after all, the epitome of security, nourishment and protection, as an evil being. Therefore the missionaries changed her from the "rebirth mother of the dead" not to the "mother of the devil", but to the "devil's grandmother". The alternative to this, which prevailed in the fairy tale, would have been the "evil stepmother".

IV 4. Hell

The Germanic tribes called their afterlife "hel", i.e. "cave" – this was the name of the burial chamber in the barrows. It became the "hell" where the devil and his grandmother lived.

Since already among the Germanic peoples themselves the afterlife goddess had begun to develop into a kind of monstrous giantess, the missionaries could well start from this motif and bring it to the fore.

The cremation burial among the Germanic tribes had led to the idea that the barrow continued to be filled with fire and embers. This could be transformed without much effort by the missionaries into a hell of fire, which really everyone had to fear …

IV 5. The Hound of Hell

The dog, which guarded every house at that time, appears of course also at the entrance to the burial chamber – and was reinterpreted by the missionaries to the hell dog, whereby they could fall back also here on first beginnings to a reinterpretation of this afterlife guard dog with the Teutons.

Probably the dog-motif was also included in this symbolism as the companion of the hunters and the shamans.

IV 6. The Demons

The image of the ancestors in the afterlife was split into two images by the missionaries – whether this was planned or just happened can hardly be determined. One of these two images were the ancestors in heaven – who were well Christianized. The other half were the ancestors in hell, who were pagan and therefore had to suffer in the tumulus fire.

These tumulus-ancestors, thus the dead spirits of the bad people in the hell ("cave") became increasingly feared beings – just demons … the entourage of the devil …

Originally "demon" has been once a designation for "soul" …

Thus, the traditional evocations of the dead were represented by the missionaries as an evocation of demons. Seeking advice and help from the deceased father was reinterpreted as a pact with the devil, in which the living person lost his soul …

The missionaries have been so thorough and so successful in no other subject as in producing the fear of evoking the spirits of the dead …

IV 7. The Worship of the Saints

The condemnation of seeking help from the ancestors naturally left a gap in the beliefs, traditions and behavior of the Germanic people. In its place, the clergy put the search for advice and help with the saints – they replaced the biological father and mother in the afterlife.

IV 8.   The Last Judgment

The Last Judgment originated with the Egyptians when they tried to resolve the contradiction between the omnipotence and justice of the gods on the one hand, and the injustice, obviously tolerated by the gods, that people committed against each other on the other hand. The solution of this contradiction could only be achieved through a judgment in the afterlife, in which the people who had done evil in their lives on earth were condemned.

This concept, which the Christians took over from the Egyptians in the form of the Last Judgment, was of course also in the background when the missionaries declared the ancestors of the Germanic tribes to be evil demons – the unbelievers became the subjects of the devil.

Thus, if someone invoked the dead, he was close to hell, the devil and eternal damnation by this act alone – for the good Christians in heaven would certainly never have obeyed such an evocation and come to the living.

It is not surprising, then, that necromancy has become the creepiest thing of all in European culture …

V   Historical examples

The following examples of evocations are far from complete, but are only a selection intended to describe the variety in which evocations occur among different peoples.

The examples are arranged chronologically.

V 1.   Neolithic Age

In Neolithic Mesopotamia there was a complex burial ritual which had three phases:

1st phase: the dead person is buried in the ground. He procreates again in the afterlife with the afterlife goddess.

2nd phase: after presumably nine months (pregnancy of the goddess with the soul of the dead man), the dead man is reborn in the afterlife. The dead man was dug up again – his bones went to a bone house, but his skull was kept in a niche in the wall inside the dwelling house of his descendants. There, his descendants could contact the dead man at any time with the help of the skull.

3rd phase: After a long period of time, presumably when no one was alive who still knew the dead person personally, the skull was also brought to the bone house.

During the 2nd phase the dead person was asked for advice and help – which can be understood as a kind of evocation, where the dead person was called into his skull.

There are also a number of skulls preserved that were covered with clay and painted to represent the dead person as real as possible. In some cases there were also sculptures that did not contain a skull.

V 2.   Egypt

After a burial, when the statue of the dead person had been completed, the Sem priest (shaman) traveled to the afterlife and retrieved the soul of the dead person in its statue so that it would be accessible to the descendants of that dead person.

This ritual is at the same time a dream journey by the Sem-priest and also an evocation of the dead person – finally the dead person is called into his statue, which is a "substitute body" for him.

The statues of the dead of the Egyptians were a more complete version of the skulls of the dead from the Neolithic period in Mesopotamia.

V 3. Sumer

In Sumer, disease spirits were evoked primarily so that they could then be expelled. This was done mainly during epidemics. So these evocations are actually exorcisms.

V 4. Hittites

The Hittites (Indo-Europeans) had shaman-priests who were responsible for after-life journeys, calling the ancestors, and evoking disease spirits during epidemics.

V 5. Romans

The Romans sometimes summoned the dead from the underworld to this world so that they could speak with them.

However, they also used evocation for military purposes: when a city was besieged, the priests summoned the gods of that city to leave and instead defect to the Romans and protect them. This tactic was also called "evocation" – an evocation of the gods rather than an evocation of the dead.

Evocation was also used to call a deity out of a temple and send it to another place – in order to be able to plunder the temple now abandoned by the gods in peace (and without fear of the revenge of the gods) …

V 6. The Witch of Endor

The "Witch of Endor" is a seeress in the Old Testament. The common expression "witch" has in the original, i.e. literally translated, the meaning "woman with divination abilities who summons the dead".

This necromancer was asked for advice by the Israeli king Saul when he received no answer from Yahweh. She then summoned the prophet Samuel, who ascended from the realm of the dead and appeared to the necromancer and King Saul. Samuel explained to Saul that Yahweh no longer answered him because Saul had not acted as God had asked of him.

V 7. Christ's Mountain Prayer

When Christ once went up a mountain with three disciples to pray, Christ shone with white light – and Moses and Elijah appeared beside Him, talking with Christ. Since these two prophets were long dead during Christ's lifetime, this is an appearance of two dead people to one living person. Since Christ went up the mountain to pray, it can be assumed that he also addressed Moses and Elijah in the process.

So, from a purely technical point of view, Christ conjured up two dead people – even though this is not normally referred to in this way in Christianity. This evocation furthermore took place in the classical way on a hill – a symbol of the burial mound.

V 8. Lazarus

Christ's raising of Lazarus from the dead, after Lazarus had been dead for some time and had already "begun to stink," is also a necromancy: Christ calls back the soul of a dead man from the afterlife and even reinserts it into his already slightly decomposed body, which then comes back to life.

V 9. Teutons

The most famous necromancy in Germanic lore will be Odin's summoning of the seeress Wala, who rose from her hillside tomb at his command. This scene is found in the "Song of Wegtam".

The shaman god Odin was also called "Lord of the Barrows" because of his necromancy.

The Germanic peoples also invoked spirits of sickness in order to drive them away – these invocations are therefore actually exorcism rituals.

V 10. Celts

In Celtic lore, the summoning of a storm spirit by the bard-druid Taliesin is most impressive.

V 11. Islam

In Islam almost the same attitude to evocations is found as in Christianity: The evocation of djinns (spirits) is forbidden, but is nevertheless carried out from time to time – what works is used.

Especially in Morocco, Oman, Saudi Arabia and the United Arab Emirates, evocations are used for revenge on the one hand and for healing on the other.

V 12. Christianity

In the Middle Ages, monks also evoked the spirits of disease in order to be able to expel them. So these evocations were also rather exorcisms.

V 13. Faust

The most famous evocation in Europe, or at least in the German-speaking world, is certainly the summoning of Mephistopheles by Faust in Goethe's drama of the same name. This representation shows above all very vividly the background for such a demon conjuration.

V 14. John Dee

John Dee contacted various angels in 1582-1587 with the help of the medium Edward Kelly, who transmitted to him the Enoch language, a magic system, and other things. This is probably the best-known example of evocation with the help of a medium.

V 15. Woodoo

The peculiarity of the evocations in Woodoo is that they are usually performed in a group and not alone or in pairs.

VI Personal Experiences

If one does not have one's own experiences on a certain subject, all conclusions drawn from other people's reports remain somewhat questionable. Everyone has to make his own experiences, but I can at least contribute some of my own experiences here.

VI 1. A Demon

My magic teacher Axel had the motto "The main thing is that it bangs and makes you dizzy!" Accordingly, I experienced quite a lot with him pretty quickly.

One day he arrived with some copies and said that he had bought the instructions for a demon summoning for quite a lot of money. This was around 1980 – at that time such instructions were not so easy to obtain. I was much too shy to say that I didn't dare to do it. So we got chalk and incense and I made a divining rod out of a hazel branch and carved it with the prescribed signs.

Then we went to a crossroads in the woods at night on the next full moon and drew the prescribed circles, triangles and symbols on the ground with chalk and waited for the church clock to strike twelve times.

Axel's shepherd dog lay in one of the circles and stayed there quietly the whole time.

After the last chime we lit the incense. I took the divining rod and read the incantation from the photocopies. (As I now know, I was holding the divining rod wrongly, i.e. upside down, like a fork). I was inwardly curious and full of fear in equal measure – I was "electrified."

Nothing happened for a while, but then I saw some red lights hovering from right to left across the woodland-way a little away. Then someone coughed several times between Axel and me in the circle where we were both standing – it was neither of us. Next there were bright blue "cracking" flashes of light up in the beech trees above us. Then, when it started to smell like sulfur and Axel said "The guy is there – I can feel him right there!" it became too much for me and I said I wanted to stop.

So I said the banishing formula and we walked back through the forest. However, the coughing of the invisible man and the smell of sulfur continued to accompany us – so I spoke the banishing formula again, whereupon it became a little quieter.

The moment when Axel and I parted in the city and I went on alone to my home was one of my worst moments – I didn't know what was about to happen. At home I locked my room (which I never did), pulled the covers over my head and hoped that it would be morning soon – I didn't sleep much that night.

In the morning I said to myself, "Either the fear gets me or I get the fear." So I went back to that spot in the woods every day I could, until after a good six months I could sit there at night and relax and think about things other than this evocation.

During this time I learned a lot about fear.

VI 2.   The Second Attempt

Since Axel really wanted to see a demon standing in front of him for once, we made a second attempt after a while, but during this attempt we encountered the forester, who found our sack with the ritual items very suspicious – he obviously thought we were poachers. So we went back home.

I believe that I brought about this failure unconsciously because I was still afraid of the appearance of a demon.

VI 3.   The Third Attempt

Axel and I carried out the third experiment in his room. The only phenomenon that occurred was that a candle in a holder on the wall received a blow so that it flew around the room.

VI 4.   A Poltergeist

When I was about 21 years old and had become Axel's "sorcerer's apprentice" for a while, I was still living with my parents. One Sunday afternoon, when I was alone in the house, sitting in my garret, I suddenly heard footsteps coming towards the house – which surprised me, because it is not possible to hear footsteps three floors below on the other side of the house on concrete slabs.

Then I heard someone opening the front door without using a key – I couldn't have heard that either, and besides, the front door was locked. Then someone came up the stairs – men's footsteps that were unfamiliar to me. By now my hair was standing on end and I looked spellbound at my bedroom door.

The footsteps came up to my door and stopped there. Then I heard someone across the hall go into my sisters' room – again the door was opened without being unlocked. Then there was silence.

After a while I told myself that I had to go and see. So I got the key to my sisters' room and looked everywhere – in all the corners, under the beds, in the wardrobes … but there was no one there.

I didn't tell anyone about it. After a few days, however, my brothers and sisters and my mother told me that they sometimes heard an invisible man running up the stairs – so I told them about my experience. After a while, all my five siblings had heard the "house ghost," as we had christened him.

Sometimes the house ghost would stand invisibly next to my second oldest sister's bed at night and tell her something, but she couldn't remember it – and she found it quite disturbing.

After a while, however, we all got used to our new roommate. When visitors came and heard the footsteps on the stairs, we said "Oh, that's just our house ghost."

Only my father had never heard him and thought we were all crazy when we told him about it.

One Sunday morning, when everyone was sitting at breakfast except me (I wasn't at home), a noise went off in my room, which was directly above the living room, as if I was smashing all my furniture with an axe. Then my father went up to my rooms in a rage and saw that there was no one there – from then on he also believed in our house ghost.

After about three quarters of a year these phenomena gradually stopped.

I suspect that they were telekinetic phenomena, which were also triggered by me, since I had suppressed my own puberty, had just learned magic, and was otherwise under a lot of internal stress. Moreover, I heard the poltergeist first and it made the loudest noise in my room.

VI 5. A Spiritistic Session

Two women who worked together with Axel in the intensive care unit of the mental hospital invited Axel and me to a spiritistic session. However, nothing much happened during this session.

Afterwards we sat together and the other three told stories about the mental hospital and about Pan – I mainly listened.

On the way home I met a woman who was obviously confused. I helped her to find her way home again. There she invited me to her apartment, where she obviously would have liked to have me in her bed, but I refused.

There apparently the spiritualistic session (calling someone), the mental hospital (confused woman) and Pan (sex) got mixed together and then crossed my path as this woman – a somewhat strange form of "evocation".

VI 6. Magic Group

A few years later Axel and I were in the "Bonn Group of Experimental Magic". There, about eight of us once invoked a Martian spirit. He was around, but he didn't show himself.

Frater Thot thought that I was blocking the appearance. Probably he was right, since in a part of me at that time I was still afraid of evocations.

VI 7. Io Pan!

A few years later Axel and I once went to a clearing in the forest and invoked the god Pan with the help of a manual Axel had procured. This evocation required several offerings and a yew wood hammer that I had made.

Pan did not appear before us, but played his flute to the left of us in the forest. There were not many notes, but something like that I have never heard again – that went through and through …

VI 8.   Runes

At about the same time, I experimented extensively with runes. I found a suitable place in the forest for each rune, stood in the rune posture, and then chanted the rune name for a long time.

After I chanted a rune on a clearing area, which was already overgrown with undergrowth, something strange happened – I think it was the "Tyr" rune, but I am not completely sure anymore.

An eagle swooped down from the sky in front of me, turned into a large snake on the ground in front of me, and then crawled away through the brush.

These two animals looked perfectly real.

A bit confused, I realized that there are no eagles in the Kottenforst and that eagles cannot turn into snakes. So this must have been a vision – an extremely real vision. It should be possible to reach this quality of the appearances also with evocations …

Of course, I asked myself, what had actually happend on that clearing. Tyr was the former father of the gods of the Germanic tribes (at the North Germanic tribes until 500 A.D.) and the eagle was at the Germanic tribes (and at all other Indo-Germanic tribes too) the soul-bird of the father of the gods. On his every evening journey to the underworld, the sun-god father of the gods, Tyr, transformed himself into a snake, which is generally the symbol of the spirits of the dead.

Did Tyr show himself to me, because I chanted his name? But why did he show me the "sunset scene", that is, his death every evening – the transformation of the sun-eagle into the underworld-serpent?

Since I sang the Tyr rune before this vision, this experience can also be counted among the evocations – although among the unintentional ones …

VI 9. Pan-Calls

Together with Axel I called Pan almost every time at the end of our meetings, which we had about twice a week, for about a year. This had been Axel's idea …

Axel stood in front of the Pan statuette that I had made out of clay and beeswax like the statuette for a Spiritus familiaris and invoked Pan with the help of Crowley's "Hymn to Pan". I improvised to this on a bamboo transverse flute, creating several "Pan themes" as I went along.

I actually had the idea that I was only supporting Axel, but had nothing to do with Pan myself – but Pan also sent me a woman who really wanted to share the bed with me …

She told me that she had intense erotic dreams about me again and again … and now she wanted to experience them in reality …

This is more generel magic than an evocation.

VI 10. Necronomicon

On another occasion Axel, Frater U.D. and I tried to summon a ghost from the Necronomicon, but nothing happened.

I suspect that this was not because the Necronomicon is a fictional book, but because I was still not quite comfortable with evocations – at least not the evocations of demons.

VI 11.   The Ghost of a Dead Man

Several years later, a friend of mine asked me if I could help a woman from the village who probably had a problem with her deceased landlord, who haunted her house and did not let the children sleep.

I went there, sat down in the children's room, lit a candle, performed the Little Pentagram Ritual internally and then summoned the deceased landlord and talked to him internally. It became clear quite quickly that he was not aware that he was dead. For the last ten years of his life he had had nothing but this house … and after his death he continued to cling to this single content of existence.

Fortunately, it was not too difficult to make him realize that he was dead and that it would make sense for him to let go of the house and go to the afterlife.

After that, things were peaceful again in the apartment.

VI 12.   Several Poltergeists

Alfter Castle, where about 30 students of an arts school had lived for a long time, had been haunted for years. After two students committed suicide there a few years apart, this haunting became much stronger. No one has been able to live in the room where one of the suicides took place.

These phenomena were strongest during the winter vacations, when only a few students were in the castle. One could almost feel someone walking next to oneself all the time. At night, these ghosts sometimes talked to the castle residents or pulled the covers off their beds. Even though most of the students got used to the ghosts quite quickly, they sometimes disturbed their sleep.

Therefore, I was invited to see if I could do something about it. However, I found that there were too many ghosts and that some of the ghosts, who had apparently been there for a few centuries, had become too strong for me. So I asked a friend who is a good psychic for help.

Together, through conversations with the spirits, through pentagram rituals, Feng Shui, petitions to Mother Earth, and the like, we finally managed to reestablish a peaceful quiet in the castle.

Basically, there is hardly any difference between a spirit summoning and a spirit banishment, i.e. between an evocation and an exorcism – at least not from the point of view of the one who performs both.

In both cases, one first seeks contact with the spirits, then speaks with them and wants something from them. Only what one wants from them is different: an advice or a help or that they go to the other world.

VI 13.   Haunting in the Bergisches Land

For some years I have often been called to haunted houses and usually it was not too difficult to restore peace. On one occasion, however, I did not succeed – although I examined the whole house and also the surrounding ruins and the like.

At that time I wondered what was actually going on in the house and where these telekinetic phenomena and this strange atmosphere came from.

A few months later, the woman who lived in the haunted house with her daughter and the woman's new boyfriend called me and told me that she had found out that her daughter was having an affair with her mother's boyfriend. The haunting phenomena were obviously telekinesis phenomena caused by the tension in the psyche of the daughter, who was about 20 years old.

VI 14.   Christ and Krishna

At about the same time I once caught a cold, but in a strange way: I merely had a severe fever (which I almost never have) and no other symptoms. Strangely enough, this fever made me physically weak but decidedly clear-headed. I was so exhausted that I had to lie in bed – but I was reading the Bhagavadgita with the stories about Krishna and Arjuna at the time.

Once when I looked up from my book and looked at my altar, I saw Christ and Krishna standing there – Christ on the left and Krishna on the right. Both were shining brightly golden and looked like brothers. The figures of the two gods were like semi-transparent images through which I could still see the background – but the two figures could be seen more clearly than the background.

This reminded me of Frater Thot's phrase "the consistency of dense vapors."

This vision or this "evocation by reading the Bhagavadgita" has been very important for me, because I had already put Christ, Krishna, Odin and all other gods and goddesses on the same level, but to see Christ and Krishna standing next to each other with the same radiance was something completely different – the theory has become experience.

As far as I know, the effect of such a vision cannot be replaced by anything else …

If one experiences such visions or evocation appearances and such things are still completely new to one and one cannot classify them at all, it can happen that one will completely forget the entire experience after two days and no longer knows anything about it – simply because one could not integrate the experience.

VI 15. Spontaneous Visit of a Dead Person

When I started working in the organic food store, I spent a month renovating a large part of the rooms, building new walls, putting in windows and doors, and the like. Since my father worked in construction (he mainly plastered ceilings), I was no stranger to these activities and knew how to handle the tools, but I had never learned these things.

One day, when I was plastering a wall, it suddenly went very quickly and very routinely and the wall was plastered in no time at all and was perfectly smooth and straight – it was as if someone had guided my hand.

Then I paused and felt around and immediately found my father who had died shortly before and who had guided my hand … Then I told him that he should "knock" next time and ask me if it was all right with me that he should take over my hand. He agreed to that.

Obviously, there are also "family constellation-like situations" where the dead come to the living of their own accord. And there is apparently also the possibility of taking over abilities of the dead.

Actually, this is a well known phenomenon: the main disciple receives the blessing and the abilities of the master at the time of death. This is not only the case with Indian gurus, but also, for example, with the prophet Elijah, who transferred his power to his disciple Elisha shortly before his death. Elisha then immediately checked if everything had worked and successfully commanded the waters of the Jordan to part and let him go dry through the riverbed to the other side.

Obviously, these transfers are also possible on a small scale and also in terms of "normal capabilities".

VI 16. The Yugoslav War

During the civil war in former Yugoslavia I lived in a small hut at the edge of the forest without water, electricity, and address. In the time when this war had begun, I had the feeling from time to time that I was not alone in the house. Then, when I looked inwardly, I usually found men who were completely lost – apparently the ghosts of dead people who had suddenly died a violent death.

I suspected that they had come into the house because I was meditating intensively there at that time and this must have been perceived by the spirits of the dead.

I was able to wake up most of the spirits from their confusion by looking them in the eyes (all inwardly, of course) and bringing them into the here and now. Sometimes, however, this was not enough – then I imagined a brightly shining, golden sun in their heart chakra to make them aware of their soul. This always worked.

After that, it was easy to send them to the otherworld.

VI 17. The Laurel Elf of La Palma

Several years ago I went with a friend to La Palma, where we wandered in the valley where the last laurel tree forest on earth is located. Since my friend at that time can not climb mountains well, she was very soon exhausted and sat down on a rock.

As I stood there looking down into the valley, the bottom of which was about 30m below me, and considering that these laurel forests had once been very widespread, I had the idea of calling the laurel forest elf. I had hardly had this thought when I already saw him – he was standing down in the valley and was so huge that we were at eye level. He didn't seem like a lovely flower spirit either, but was stocky and robust and a bit restrained, a 35m tall giant, though at the same time, well, I can best describe it as "life friendly".

I greeted him and asked him if he could give my friend some strength to keep walking. He nodded, glanced briefly at her, and then continued up the valley.

My perception was like a dream journey with open eyes, where the inner and outer images overlay each other and the image coming from the inside is semi-transparent.

My friend clearly felt the "blessing" of the laurel elf (she did not know that I had just seen him) and actually felt fit again and instead of turning back we were able to walk up the valley for another half hour.

That was a very simple evocation …

VI 18. Family Constellations

I have already conducted several family constellations. Again and again, the variety of details that the people who represent a deceased person know about this deceased person is revealed – simply because they embody him or her in the constellation.

Here "complex telepathy" and the presence of the spirit in the performer cannot be distinguished in the end. It is merely evident that the performer can connect with the deceased simply by choosing to do so – a very simple evocation … or rather invocation.

VI 19. Pan

Once, a few years ago, I was riding my bicycle home from swimming in a lake and I didn't want to be alone anymore, I wanted to have a girlfriend again. I then inwardly said this to Pan.

When I arrived home, a woman from Holland called me and told me that she had read a book of mine and since then had erotic dreams about me and would like to meet me and that she was thinking about having a child with me …

But that was a bit too much and too fast for me – and the woman didn't sound really sympathetic to me either.

It seems to be Pan's method to send erotic dreams to a person, if a magician or a witch asks Pan for help for an erotic adventure, so that this "dreamer" then absolutely wants to share her bed with the magician or witch. I have already experienced the same procedure about 30 years before with the Pan invocations with Axel.

VII   Aids for an Evocation

Evocations can be performed very simply, but also with complex rituals. This is on the one hand a question of style and on the other hand it also depends on the tradition in which the person stands and on the circumstances.

VII 1.   The Grave

If one wants to evoke a certain spirit of the dead, it is obvious to do this at the grave of the person concerned – just as it was customary in former times among the Indo-Germanic peoples and others to call out the dead from their burial mounds.

VII 2.   The Cross-Roads

The crossroads, was already a popular place of worship among the Germanic peoples. Since the sun symbol was a circle with a cross in it (horizon-circle and four directions) and the Tyr, the god of the dead, was also a sun god, the offerings to Tyr were partly laid down at crossroads.

Since Tyr as a sun god died every evening, the crossroads was apparently also associated with the dead and then finally also with necromancy. It is possible that later an association with the Christian cross also played a role.

In general, the place where two lines cross is a point of concentration – and therefore also suitable for the calling of a spirit.

VII 3.   Midnight

The time "midnight" is suitable for evocations because night has been associated with the afterlife – "midnight" is also called "dead of night".

Successful evocations are of course possible at any place and at any time.

VII 4.   Circle and Triangle

The circle is the protection symbol for the magician and the triangle in front of this circle is the "prison" for the evoked spirit, which it cannot leave.

However, I have also heard from an acquaintance that he drew the triangle into the circle and not in front of the circle – this also worked …

VII 5.   Magic Signs

The signs painted around the circle and sometimes around the triangle are symbols of deities, spirits, angels, demons, etc., which are supposed to protect the circle and keep the spirit inside the triangle.

VII 6.   Candles

Some instructions say that candles should be lit. However, they do not seem to have any special meaning.

VII 7.   Oils

Sometimes the candles are smeared with consecrated oil, which makes them a symbol of protection – the power of consecration in the oil smeared on the candles spreads in the circle or around the circle when the candles are burned.

VII 8.   Incense

Burned incense is said to release life force, which the spirits can then use to become visible and possibly even partially materialize.

The Egyptians called incense "senetjer", meaning "that which makes divine" in the sense of "that which calls the deity or spirit of the dead to his statue". Thus, the use of incense in evocations has a long tradition.

Axel and I once considered whether the spirits might need a lot of smoke, that they can use to telekinetically form their bodies from this smoke. So we performed an evocation where we placed about 50 incense cones on plates on which we had previously placed wax remnants.

The smoke became extremely violent, but the effect was merely that we could hardly breathe and had to tear open the door and windows …

VII 9. Talismans and Amulets

Sometimes consecrated objects are used by the necromancer to protect himself from the spirits. These can be very different things, depending on the tradition.

VII 10. Magic Wand and Divining Rod

The magic wand was originally the scepter of the seers. It symbolized the world tree that connected this world on earth with the otherworld in heaven. The world tree was, so to speak, the way of work of the seers.

In the course of time, the staff has been reinterpreted from a symbol of the seers' activity to the vessel of the seers' power.

In more recent times, the wands have sometimes been hollowed out and filled with a "magical substance". This method has become quite popular again through the "Harry Potter" books.

The divining rod is actually used for finding things that lie underground, but sometimes it appears in the evocation instructions instead of a wand – a confusion which, however, does not prevent the evocation from being successful …

VII 11. Texts

The spirits and especially the demons are often invoked with traditional texts. They can consist of two to three sentences or be very long.

However, one can also call the spirits with freely improvised words – as it is common e.g. with African medicine men.

VII 12.   Invocation of the Gods

In most evocations that originated within a monotheistic culture, the magician first invokes God, then the archangels, then the angels, etc., claiming at least that he is acting on behalf of the Most High: "In the name of …(God)… I command you, … (spirit)…, that you …"

The magician follows the prescribed official path and thereby receives his authority "from on high" and is therefore in a position to command the demons.

VII 13.   Demon Names

If a concrete dead person or a concrete demon (who is responsible for a certain task) is evoked, the use of the name of this dead person or demon is natural.

It is like dialing the right phone number or typing the right internet address …

VII 14.   Gestures

In the Occident, only a few gestures are used in evocations. The magician sometimes raises his arms to invoke the protection of the gods and he indicates to the demon with his wand his place in the triangle in front of the circle.

VII 15.   Dances

Dances in evocations are found more in Africa or Woodoo than in the European tradition.

There are special dances for this purpose in Africa, accompanied by songs and drums. These dances are performed before festivals, inviting the dead, who then come to the village from the bush ("otherworld"). In this context, the evocation is not at all sinister, but filled with the joy of feeling the spirits of the deceased ancestors around you again.

For these ancestral invocations, the large ritual drums ("yokoto") are used, which have a very deep sound.

VII 16. Sacrifices

Sacrifices have the same function as the burning of incense: the life force released is to facilitate the appearance of the spirit. Besides, a sacrifice also makes an evocation special – after all, one cannot sacrifice at random.

These sacrifices range from burning incense to food and drink to the sacrifice of animals and humans or simply of some drops of one's own blood.

Human sacrifices, however, are known only from earlier cults in Europe and America and only in connection with oracles and the summoning of deities. The dead were not summoned with the help of human sacrifices – that would have been a bit contradictory …

VIII   What is an Evocation?

After the reflections in this book, one can ask the question of the first chapter again and see what can be said about it.

It can be stated quite simply that in an evocation one calls a spirit and then speaks with it. However, it is considerably less easy to say what exactly happens in the process. It is even more difficult to find out when and why an evocation works – and when and why it does not.

VIII 1.   What happens during an Evocation?

During an evocation, the magician sees and hears (and smells) a spirit.

If several people see this spirit at the same time, these people are at least telepathically coupled with each other as in a group dream journey. On a group dream journey several people are in the same inner picture and see the same things before the first of them expresses what he sees. It is apparently also possible to see this inner image collectively on the outside – that is, the inner image is collectively superimposed on the visual perception of the environment.

If the outer image can also be photographed, then either there really is something in the outside or the image has come onto the film by telekinesis.

In the end there is nothing by which one could decide the question "On the inseide or on the outside?" with certainty, because in the end there is just nothing else than the perceptions.

Therefore one can say that an evoked spirit or a spirit-appearance can have the same reality as every other perception. With this one still does not know what a spirit is, which appeared at an evocation – but one does not know that much more certainly about an apple.

If a materialization occurs at the evocation, the normal world view, which is limited to the matter, is anyway overtaxed, because such a phenomenon should not occur at all according to the normal world view.

Then one doesn't need to ask any more about the "material reality" of the evoked spirit …

VIII 2. What can an Evocation look like?

A spirit can turn out to be telekinesis – as in the case of the pubertal poltergeist.

A spirit can be always present – as with the skulls in the dwelling house in the Neolithic.

A spirit can already be there – as with a haunted house.

A spirit can come on its own – like my father who helped me plaster the wall.

A spirit can appear to you as in an everyday encounter – like the laurel elf.

A spirit can feel called by a song – as with my eagle/snake vision.

A spirit can show up in a medium – as in a family constellation.

A spirit can be summoned through engagement with it – as with my vision of Christ and Krishna.

A spirit can be summoned through a meditation – as in Christ's transfiguration when Moses and Elijah appeared.

A spirit can be summoned through a dream journey – as in the Egyptian burial ritual.

A spirit can be called forth from its grave – as in the "utiseta" of the Germanic peoples.

A spirit can be summoned – a s in a ritual evocation.

A spirit can be summoned from a collective prayer – a in an apparition of Mary.

A spirit can be called by a group – as in a spiritistic session.

A spirit can be called with great force – as in an exorcism.

- - -

As this overview shows, evocations can look very diverse: from the spirit that is always present anyway, to the spirit that must be called with emphasis.

Also the mood of the evocation can be very different: from "familiar" with the ancestor spirit in his skull in the living room, to "curious" with the family constellations, to "creepy" with the evocation at night in the cemetery.

Likewise, the reason for the evocation can range from curiosity to the intention to heal to greed for power.

VIII 3. When is an Evocation successful?

Some evocations succeed unintentionally – others do not succeed even with a lot of effort … this does not make it easy to know when an evocation works.

Besides, many things happen that one did not expect: floating lights, coughing of invisible people, light explosions in tree tops, smell of sulfur, materializations, appearances of gods … this is rather confusing and unpredictable.

Nevertheless, it can be said that a certain single-mindedness is conducive – no matter whether it happens out of fear, out of greed for power, out of an "en passant wish", out of being firmly rooted in a tradition or out of the coincidental fulfillment of all preconditions of an evocation (as in the case of chanting the name "Tyr").

This corresponds to what can be observed elsewhere in magic – the relaxed, contradiction-free one-pointedness has the greatest magical effect.

IX   Why Evocations?

Finally, one should also ask the question of when an evocation is useful. The following reasons are likely to be the most common:

If one is curious about the experience itself, there is no way around an evocation of one's own.

If one wants to obtain information in a magical way, a dream journey is sufficient – in this way telepathy can be practiced quite easily.

If you want to get in touch with a spirit or a deity, a dream journey is also the easiest way.

If you want to achieve such a contact as a group, the dream journey is also preferable. However, with more then a dozen people, the evocation would be more practical, because the coordination of those present becomes easier than on a dream journey, where you are traveling with 50 people in the same inner image …

If one is looking for help, a simple ritual is enough, in which one addresses a deity, but does not evoke it.

- - -

Thus remain as reason for an evocation on the one hand the curiosity and on the other hand the cult, in which many people are involved.

X   The Evocation of the Angantyr

One of the most dramatic descriptions of an evocation of the dead is found among the Germanic tribes in the "Saga of Hervor and King Heidrek the Wise".

Hervor is a king's daughter who disguises herself as a man and commands a Viking dragon ship. She largely has the character of a Valkyrie.

Then Hervor prepared to go off on her own in the clothes and with the weapons of a man. She came to a place where there were some Vikings and sailed with them for a time. She called herself Hervard during this time.

A little later, the captain died and this 'Hervard' took command of the crew. And when they came to the island of Samsey, 'Hervard' told them to stop there so he could go up onto the island and said there'd be a good chance of treasure in the mound. But all the crewmen speak against it and say that such evil things walk there night and day that it's worse there in the daytime than most places are at night.

In the end, they agree to drop anchor, and 'Hervard' climbed into the boat and rowed ashore and landed in Munway just as the sun was setting.

And he met a man there watching his herd.

The young maiden
met at sunset
in Munway Cove
a man herding.

He said:

"Of human kind,
who's come to the island?
Hie you hastily
home to your lodging!"

She said:

"Home to my lodging
I'll hie me not,
as I know none
of the island folk;
so inform me fast
before you go:
where are Hjorvard's
Howes meant to be?"

He said:

"Don't ask me that,
you don't seem wise,
prince of pirates,
your plight is dire;
let's flee as fast
as our feet can carry us;
it's all too much
for men out here."

She said:

"Here's a prize necklace
in payment for talk;
I doubt you'll divert
the vikings' leader"

He said:

"None can hand me
such hansom gems,
such good treasures
that I go not my way."

She spoke:

"Let us not be so easily frightened
by that little hiss and crackle,
not even when the whole island
flares up in fire;
let's not take fright
at fallen heroes
quite so quickly,
come let us talk."

He said:

"Silly would seem
someone to me
who heads on alone
from here by night;
fire is blazing,
barrows open,
field burns and fen –
let's go faster."

Hotfoot to the holt
the herdsman was off then,
fled far away
from the words of this girl,
but Hervor's heart
hard-knit in her breast
swells boldly now
about such matters.

And so he took off home to his village, and they parted company there. And at that she sees where the grave-fire is burning over on the edge of the island, and she goes up there and is not afraid though all the mounds were in her path and the dead standing outside. She waded through the flame as if through fog till she came to the barrow of the berserks.

Hervor's father Angantyr and her grandfather Arngrim had been leaders of berserkers and berserkers themselves.

According to the ideas of the Germanic people, fire blazed at night from the tumuli graves, where a spirit of the dead still dwelt.

Then she called:

"Awake, Angantyr!
Hervor wakes you,
only daughter
of you and Svafa;
from your crypt give me
that keenest blade,
the sword dwarves struck
for King Sigrlami.

Hervard, Hjorvard,
Hrani, Angantyr,
under forest roots
I rouse you all,
with buckler, with byrnie,
bright helm and harness,
a good sharp glaive,
and gold-reddened spear.

A glefe is a long staff with a long knife attached to the front. The glefe is a simple form of the halberd, a "knife spear" so to speak.

Eyfura is the mother of Hervor's father Angantyr. "Eyfura's boy" is therefore Angantyr.

So much for you
sons of Arngrim,
mean men
to the mould adding,
when Eyfura's boy
won't even talk
to me tonight
in Munway Bay.

Hervard, Hjorvard,
Hrani, Angantyr,
be racked in your ribs
as if rotting
deep in an anthill,
if you don't hand over
Dvalin's sword;
it does not suit
dead men to grip
a good weapon."

Then said Angantyr:

"Hervor, daughter,
what drives you to call so?
Brimful of bale-runes,
you're bound for grief.
You're out of your mind,
mad have you gone,
lost your wits now,
waking up dead men.

A father did not
dig my grave,
no parent buried me,
nor other kinsmen;
they had Tyrfing,
the two who lived,
though the owner was
but one in the end."

The sword „Tyrfing" ("Finger of Tyr") originally has been the magical sword of Tyr.

She said:

"It's a lie what you say—
may the god only let you
sit hale in your howe
if you have not got it
laid in there with you;
reluctant you are
heirlooms to share
with your only child."

Then the mound opened and it was as though the whole barrow was fire and flame.

And Angantyr said:

"The gate to Hel gapes
and graves open,
all is fire
on the island's rim;
it's grim outside
to gaze around;
shift yourself, girl,
if you can, to your ships."

She answers:

"You can't burn
any bonfires by night,
no flames flaring
to frighten me;
your daughter's mind
does not tremble
though dead men there
in the door she sees."

Then said Angantyr:

"I say to you, Hervor,
have a listen,
wise daughter, now
to what will be:
this sword Tyrfing
(try to believe it)
will, girl, your offspring
all destroy.

A lad you'll bear
who later shall own
the sword Tyrfing
and trust his own strength;
people will call
the boy Heidrek,
he'll grow mightiest
under heaven's tent."

She declared:

"I cast this curse
on killed warriors,
that you entombed
shall all lie there
undead with dead
in the dank rotten;
give me, Angantyr,
from out of your mound
(it won't help you to hide it)
the dwarves' handiwork."

The magical sword of Tyr was made by his two sons ("Alcis"), wo later became dwarves.

He says:

"I say you aren't, girl,
like other humans,
to walk among howes
up here by night
with graven spear
and with Gothic steel,
with helm and harness
at the door to my hall."

Then said Hervor:

"I did think I was human,
at home with the living,
till down I came
to your dead men's hall;
so hand me from your howe
what hates armour,
the hazard of shields,
Hjalmar's bane."

that which hates armor (shatters) = sword
spoiling of shields = shield
Hjalmar's misfortune = the sword Tyrfing, by which Hjalmar was killed.

Then said Angantyr:

"Hjalmar's bane lies
below my shoulders;
the blade is wrapped
right round in flame;
one girl only
on earth up there
I guess would dare
take that glaive in hand."

Hjalmar's misfortune = the sword with which Hjalmar was killed.
glaive = sword

Hervor said:

"I'll take care of
and take in my hand
edge-sharp the blade,
could I but have it;
I'm not afraid
of fire burning;
the flame's soon out
that I look over."

Then said Angantyr:

"You're foolish, Hervor,
but full of daring,
to rush into fire
with your eyes open;
rather, young girl,
I think I'll give you
the cleaver from my cairn,
I can't refuse."

Hervor said:

"You did well,
warrior kinsman,
when from your grave
you gave the sword;
I'd rather have that,
regal lord,
than all Norway
beneath my sway."

Angantyr said:

"Wicked woman,
what would you know?
No need for glee
or glad words now;
this blade Tyrfing
(you'd better believe)
will, girl, your offspring
all destroy."

She says:

"I will go
to my ocean-steeds;
now the chief's daughter
is cheery enough;
what do I care,
cousin of nobles,
how later my sons
will settle this thing."

He says:

"You shall own
and long enjoy,
but keep covered,
what killed Hjalmar;
press not the edges—
there's poison in both—
a man's doom, that,
more dire than plague.

Fare well, daughter,
freely I'd have lent you
the lives of twelve men,
could you believe,
strength and stoutness,
all the sturdy vigour
that Arngrim's lads
left when they died."

She said:

"Now rest you all
(I'm raring to go)
hale men in your mound;
for a moment there I almost
thought I trod
between the worlds
when all about me
fires burned."

The reforging of the Tyr sword in the underworld and the return of the sun god father Tyr, reborn in the morning by the otherworld goddess, has here become the fetching of the Tyr sword from the hill grave by a kind of Valkyrie woman.

Then she went to the ships. But when it got light, she saw that the ships were gone. The vikings had taken fright at the thunders and fires on the island. She gets herself passage from there but nothing is known of her journey till she comes to Godmund in Glasisvellir, and she stayed there over winter and still called herself Hervard.

English Books by Harry Eilenstein

- Living Magic (261 p.)	- Mandalas for Beginners
- The Synthesis of Physics and Magic (192 p.)	- Money Magic for Beginners
- Astral Projection for Beginners (60 p.)	- Love Magic for Beginners
- Invocations for Beginners (52 p.)	- Magic Research for Beginners
- Evocations for Beginners (62 p.)	- Self-awareness for Beginners
- Auto-Movement for Beginners (60 p.)	- Symbolism of Numbers for Beginners
- Elves for Beginners (56 p.)	- Language of the Moon – for Beginners
These books will be puplished soon:	- Magic Chant for Beginners
- Telepathy for Beginners	- Prophecy for Beginners
- Telepathy for Advanced Learners	- Shamanism for Beginners
- Telekinesis for Beginners	- Magic Objects for Beginners
- Life Force for Beginners	- Da'ath-Magic for Beginners
- Meditation for Beginners	- Crop Circles for Beginners
- Kundalini for Beginners	- Feng Shui for Beginners
- Hypnosis for Beginners	- Magic for Beginners – Anthology I
- Chakra-Magic for Beginners	- Magic for Beginners – Anthology II
- Astrology for Beginners	- Magic for Beginners – Anthology III
- Ritual Magic for Beginners	- Magic for Beginners – Anthology IV

Bücher von Harry Eilenstein

Religion allgemein
- Die sieben Schritte des Lebens (428 S.)
- Muttergöttin und Schamanen (168 S.)
- Göbekli Tepe (472 S.)
- Die Göttin von Göbekli Tepe (144 S.)
- Totempfähle (440 S.)
- Christus (60 S.)
- Dakini (80 S.)
- Vajra (76 S.)

Ägypten
- Hathor und Re 1: Götter und Mythen im Alten Ägypten (432 S.)
- Hathor und Re 2: Die altägyptische Religion – Ursprünge, Kult und Magie (396 S.)
- Isis (508 S.)

Indogermanen
- Die Entwicklung der indogermanischen Religionen (700 S.)
- Wurzeln und Zweige der indogermanischen Religion (224 S.)

Germanen
- Die Götter der Germanen (87 Bände – siehe nächste Seite)
- Odin (300 S.)

Kelten
- Cernunnos (690 S.)
- Taliesin (228 S.)
- Der Kessel von Gundestrup (220 S.)
- Der Chiemsee-Kessel (76)

Psychologie
- Über die Freude (100 S.)
- Das Geheimnis des inneren Friedens (252 S.)
- Das Beziehungsmandala (52 S.)
- Gefühle und ihre Verwandlungen (404 S.)
- einsgerichtet (140 S.)
- Liebe und Eigenständigkeit (216 S.)
- Von innerer Fülle zu äußerem Gedeihen (52 S.)

Heilung
- Die Symbolik der Krankheiten (76 S.)

Kunst
- Herz des Tanzes – Tanz des Herzens (160 S.)

Drama
- König Athelstan (104 S.)

Bücher von Harry Eilenstein

„Magie für Anfänger"

- Telepathie für Anfänger (60 S.)
- Telepathie für Fortgeschrittene (52 S.)
- Telekinese für Anfänger (52 S.)
- Lebenskraft für Anfänger (60 S.)
- Meditation für Anfänger (56 S.)
- Kundalini für Anfänger (100 S.)
- Hypnose für Anfänger (56 S.)
- Auto-Movement für Anfänger (56 S.)
- Chakra-Magie für Anfänger (148 S.)
- Astralreisen für Anfänger (56 S.)
- Astrologie für Anfänger (120 S.)
- Ritual-Magie für Anfänger (56 S.)
- Mandalas für Anfänger (68 S.)
- Geldzauber für Anfänger (56 S.)
- Liebeszauber für Anfänger (52 S.)
- Invokationen für Anfänger (52 S.)
- Evokationen für Anfänger (60 S.)
- Elfen für Anfänger (56 S.)
- Magie-Forschung für Anfänger (140 S.)
- Selbsterkenntnis für Anfänger (52 S.)
- Zahlensymbolik für Anfänger (60 S.)
- Die Sprache des Mondes – für Anfänger (116 S.)
- Zaubergesänge für Anfänger (100 S.)
- Zukunftschau für Anfänger (60 S.)
- Schamanismus für Anfänger (52 S.)
- Magische Gegenstände für Anfänger (68 S.)
- Da'ath-Magie für Anfänger (64 S.)
- Kornkreise für Anfänger (348 S.)
- Feng Shui für Anfänger (96 S.)
- Magie für Anfänger – Sammelband I (696 S.)
- Magie für Anfänger – Sammelband II (664 S.)
- Magie für Anfänger – Sammelband III (580 S.)

„Traumreisen"

- Traumreisen zu Heilpflanzen (700 S.)

Magie

- Handbuch für Zauberlehrlinge (408 S.)
- Tarot (104 S.)
- Physik und Magie (184 S.)
- Die Synthese von Physik und Magie (200S.)
- Die Magie-Formel (156 S.)
- Krafttiere – Tiergöttinnen – Tiertänze (112 S.)
- Schwitzhütten (524 S.)
- Mythen und Magie der Harfe (116 S.)
- Magie heute – Berichte aus der Praxis (288 S.)

Meditation

- Der Lebenskraftkörper (230 S.)
- Die Chakren (100 S.)
- Das Chakren-System mit den Nebenchakren (296 S.)
- Organe und Chakren (64 S.)
- Die platonischen Körper in den Chakren (156 S.)
- Meditation (140 S.)
- Drachenfeuer (124 S.)
- Kundalini I (676 S.)
- Reinkarnation (156 S.)
- einsgerichtet (140 S.)

Astrologie

- Astrologie (496 S.)
- Photo-Astrologie (428 S.)
- Die astrologischen Aspekte (88 S.)
- Horoskop und Seele (120 S.)

Kabbala

- Kursus der praktischen Kabbala (150 S.)
- Eltern der Erde (450 S.)
- Blüten des Lebensbaumes:
    - Die Struktur des kabbalistischen Lebensbaumes (370 S.)
    - Der kabbalistische Lebensbaum als Forschungshilfsmittel (580 S.)
    - Der kabbalistische Lebensbaum als spirituelle Landkarte (520 S.)

Die Themen der 87 Bände der Reihe „Die Götter der Germanen"

1. Die Entwicklung der germanischen Religion
2. Lexikon der germanischen Religion
3. Der ursprüngliche Göttervater Tyr
4. Tyr in der Unterwelt: der Schmied Wieland
5. Tyr in der Unterwelt: der Riesenkönig   Teil 1
6. Tyr in der Unterwelt: der Riesenkönig   Teil 2
7. Tyr in der Unterwelt: der Zwergenkönig
8. Der Himmelswächter Heimdall
9. Der Sommergott Baldur
10. Der Meeresgott: Ägir, Hler und Njörd
11. Der Eibengott Ullr
12. Die Zwillingsgötter Alcis
13. Der neue Göttervater Odin   Teil 1
14. Der neue Göttervater Odin   Teil 2
15. Der Fruchtbarkeitsgott Freyr
16. Der Chaos-Gott Loki
17. Der Donnergott Thor
18. Der Priestergott Hönir
19. Die Göttersöhne
20. Die unbekannteren Götter
21. Die Göttermutter Frigg
22. Die Liebesgöttin: Freya und Menglöd
23. Die Erdgöttinnen
24. Die Korngöttin Sif
25. Die Apfel-Göttin Idun
26. Die Hügelgrab-Jenseitsgöttin Hel
27. Die Meeres-Jenseitsgöttin Ran
28. Die unbekannteren Jenseitsgöttinnen
29. Die unbekannteren Göttinnen
30. Die Nornen
31. Die Walküren
32. Die Zwerge
33. Der Urriese Ymir
34. Die Riesen
35. Die Riesinnen
36. Mythologische Wesen
37. Mythologische Priester und Priesterinnen
38. Sigurd/Siegfried
39. Helden und Göttersöhne
40. Die Symbolik der Vögel und Insekten
41. Die Symbolik der Schlangen, Drachen und Ungeheuer
42.a Die Symbolik der Herdentiere I
42.b Die Symbolik der Herdentiere II
43. Die Symbolik der Raubtiere
44. Die Symbolik der Wassertiere und sonstigen Tiere
45. Die Symbolik der Pflanzen
46. Die Symbolik der Farben
47. Die Symbolik der Zahlen
48. Die Symbolik von Sonne, Mond und Sternen
49.a Das Jenseits I – Das Hügelgrab
49.b Das Jenseits II – Der Jenseitsweg
50. Seelenvogel, Utiseta und Einweihung
51. Wiederzeugung und Wiedergeburt
52. Elemente der Kosmologie
53. Der Weltenbaum
54. Die Symbolik der Himmelsrichtungen und der Jahreszeiten
55.a Mythologische Motive I
55.b Mythologische Motive II
56. Der Tempel
57. Die Einrichtung des Tempels
58. Priesterin – Seherin – Zauberin – Hexe
59. Priester – Seher – Zauberer
60. Rituelle Kleidung und Schmuck
61. Skalden und Skaldinnen
62   Kriegerinnen und Ekstase-Krieger
63. Die Symbolik der Körperteile
64.a Magie und Ritual I
64.b Magie und Ritual II
64.c Magie und Ritual III
65. Gestaltwandlungen
66.a Magische Angriffs-Waffen
66.b Magische Verteidigungs-Waffen
67. Magische Werkzeuge und Gegenstände
68. Zaubersprüche
69. Göttermet
70. Zaubertränke
71. Träume, Omen und Orakel
72. Runen
73. Sozial-religiöse Rituale
74. Weisheiten und Sprichworte
75. Kenningar
76. Rätsel
77. Die vollständige Edda des Snorri Sturluson
78. Frühe Skaldenlieder
79.a Mythologische Sagas I
79.b Mythologische Sagas II
80. Hymnen an die germanischen Götter